REBELS WITH A CAUSE

REVOLUTIONARIES

By Paul Thomas

 Belitha Press

First published in Great Britain in 1997 by

  Belitha Press Limited,
London House, Great Eastern Wharf
Parkgate Road, London SW11 4NQ

Copyright in this format © Belitha Press Limited 1997
Text copyright © Paul Thomas

Editor: Veronica Ross
Series designer: Hayley Cove
Picture researcher: Diana Morris
Consultant: Hazel Mary Martell
Cover Illustrator: Mac McIntosh

ISBN 1 85561 551 7

Printed in Portugal

British Library Cataloguing in Publication Data
CIP data for this book is available from the British Library.

Photographic credits
AKG, London: 7t,10;12b *Bonaparte Crossing the Alps,*1800 by J.L. David, Schloss
Charlottenburg, Berlin; 15t Musée Carnavalet, Paris; 15b private collection; 20, 24.
Bridgeman Art Library: 6 *Portrait of Samuel Adams,* Anon, Museum of Fine Arts, Boston; 8b
Portrait of George Washington by James the Elder Peale, (1749-1831) Christies, London;
11t *Slaves Fell the Ripe Sugar, Antigua,* 1823 (print) by W. Clark (fl.1823) British Library,
London; 32 *In the Winter Palace* by Caroll N. Jones, Jnr. (20th century), Forbes Magazine
Collection, London; 41t *Men of the South,* 1921 by Sean Keating (1880-1977), Crawford
Municipal Art Gallery, Cork. Camera Press: 5t. Corbis-Bettmann: 27t, 29b. E.T. Archive: 12t;
14 Musée Carnavalet, Paris; 16t; 16b Musée Carnavalet, Paris; 19t Panteon Naçional;
19b; 27b George Eastman House; 28, 37t. Mary Evans Picture Library: 4, 13, 45b. Hulton
Getty Picture Collection: 11b, 17, 18, 21b, 22, 23t, 26, 29t, 31t, 31bl, 31br, 33t, 33b,
34, 35b, 38, 39t, 39b, 40, 41b, 42, 43t, 43b, 44. David King Collection: 30, 45t. Peter
Newark's Pictures: 7b, 8t, 9, 23b, 35t, 36. Only Horses Picture Agency: 37b. Frank
Spooner Pictures/Gamma/F. Anderson 5b. Tony Stone Images: 25.

Words in **bold** appear in the glossary on page 46.

CONTENTS

INTRODUCTION

Throughout history, men and women have rebelled against their circumstances and fought for changes in the way countries are governed. In this book, we look at the role played by ten people who struggled to change society.

World revolutions

There have been few great revolutions in world history, but their impact is far-reaching. One of the most famous is the French Revolution of 1789, led by Danton and Robespierre, which replaced the French monarchy with a **republic**.

Freedom and equality

The success of the French Revolution, and the new society in which all men were free and equal inspired Simón Bolívar's fight for independence in South America. In Haiti, Toussaint L'Ouverture, was also encouraged by the French Revolution. He won freedom for the slaves and independence for the island.

American rebels

Samuel Adams was one of the great leaders of the American Revolution, a struggle for independence which led to the creation of the United States of America in 1776.

Later on in American history we read about two revolutionaries who fought the American government. One is the Native American Geronimo, who struggled to protect his traditional way of life, and the other the anarchist Emma Goldman.

Russian revolutionaries attacking police headquarters in 1917.

The twentieth century

Some of the most dramatic revolutions in history happened this century. In 1917, Lenin led the revolt against the Russian empire, and founded the first **communist** country in the world. Zapata went to war against the Mexican landowners; Michael Collins fought against British rule in Ireland, and Mao Zedong defeated all opposition to become the leader of China.

Revolutions will continue to happen whenever people feel they must try to fight brutal governments to demand freedom and justice. But not all revolutions are successful. In 1956, thousands of Hungarians who marched in peaceful protest against communist rule were massacred. In 1989, more than 1000 Chinese students were killed when they gathered in Tiananmen Square, Beijing, to demand government reforms.

The tanks move into Budapest, Hungary's capital city, to crush the uprising of 1956.

Chinese students surrounded by soldiers in Tiananmen Square.

SAMUEL ADAMS

1722–1803

Samuel Adams was one of the great heroes of the American Revolution, which freed America from British rule and led to the creation of the United States of America.

In the seventeenth century, English **pioneers** set sail for North America and set up **colonies** along the eastern coast. These small settlements grew as more and more people **emigrated** to America, and by the eighteenth century, Britain ruled 13 colonies. Each colony had its own local government, but all the important decisions were made in Britain. The settlers were not happy with this situation. They wanted to rule themselves without any interference from Britain.

A career in politics

Samuel Adams was born in 1722 in Boston, Massachusetts to a wealthy brewing family. He went to Harvard College to study law, and wanted to become a politician. As a young man, Adams supported the growing movement to free the colonies from British rule. He was particularly angry that the colonies were forced to pay **taxes** to the British government.

Revolutionary leader Samuel Adams persuaded Americans to support the fight for freedom from British control.

New responsibilities

In 1748, Adams' father died, leaving Samuel to care for his mother, and the family business. But Adams' political activities made it impossible for him to look after the brewery. Before long the business started to lose money, and Adams found himself hopelessly in debt. Adams' **creditors** tried to force him to sell his home so that he could pay off his debts. But Adams fought back and threatened to **prosecute** any creditors who dared set foot on his property. Then in 1757, a tragedy occurred – Adams' wife Elizabeth died, and Adams was left to look after his two young children, Hannah and Samuel.

The Boston Massacre

On 5 March 1770, an angry crowd of Americans came upon eight British soldiers guarding a public

building in Boston. After some pushing and shoving, someone yelled 'Fire!' The soldiers fired their guns, and four Americans were shot dead.

The following day, the newspapers described the event as the 'Boston Massacre'. It was not clear who started the fight, but the incident angered many Americans and made them determined to join the struggle for independence.

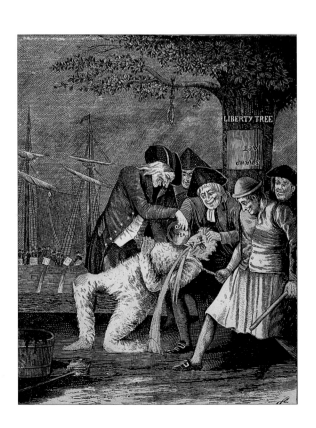

The Stamp Act

In spite of these events, Adams carried on with his political activities. In 1765, he helped to fight the Stamp Act. This was a British tax that demanded extra payment on books, newspapers, and all types of legal documents. The protesters set up a society called the Sons of Liberty, and held meetings at the giant Liberty Tree in Boston. Eventually, the protesters were successful and the Stamp Act was repealed, which meant that it was no longer law.

A political cartoon showing American rebels forcing British tea into the mouth of a tax collector in protest at British taxes. The tax collector has been **tarred and feathered**. The Stamp Act is nailed upside down to the Liberty Tree.

The Boston Tea Party

One of the most unpopular British taxes was one on tea. On 16 December 1773, a group of protesters, dressed as Native Americans and wearing war paint and feathers, boarded a British ship in Boston harbour. They forced open 342 chests of tea and emptied the contents into the water. This incident became known as the Boston Tea Party.

The British government reacted by closing Boston harbour. Neither the Americans or the British were prepared to **negotiate**. Many people thought that there would soon be war, and the colonists began to build up supplies of weapons.

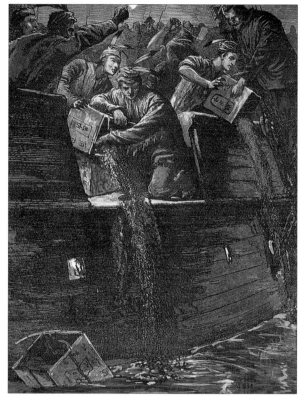

American rebels raiding a British ship and throwing the cargo of tea into the Boston harbour. Other tea parties soon happened all over America.

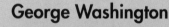

George Washington

General George Washington became the leader of the colonists' army in 1775. He believed that the Americans had no choice but to fight for freedom from British rule. His courage and determination spurred the rebels on until the American Revolution finally ended in 1781.

Washington became a national hero. He was elected the first President of the United States in 1789, and served for two four-year terms of office. America's capital city, Washington DC, was named in his honour.

War begins

On 16 April 1775, British soldiers seized a supply of guns held by colonists at Concord, Massachusetts. Shooting broke out, and within seconds eight Americans lay dead. War was declared, and the American fight for independence began.

The Declaration of Independence

The 13 colonies set up the Congress of American Colonies, and appointed George Washington as commander-in-chief of its army. Under his leadership the Americans fought against British troops for more than a year. Then, on 4 July 1776, the Congress of Colonies passed the Declaration of Independence, which said that all 13 colonies were independent and free from British rule. Adams' signature was ninth on this important document.

The Peace of Paris

Five years of fighting followed until British troops were forced to surrender to the colonists at Yorktown in 1781. Two years later in 1783, a peace conference in Paris recognized the independence of the colonies, or the United States of America.

State governor

After the war, Adams became governor of Massachusetts, but he retired from public life in 1798. Towards the end of his life, he wrote 'I thank God that I have lived to see my country independent and free.' Samuel Adams died in Boston in 1803.

A painting by John Trumbull showing American revolutionary leaders signing the Declaration of Independence.

TOUSSAINT L'OUVERTURE

1743–1803

In the 1790s, rebel leader Toussaint L'Ouverture and his army of slaves rose up in revolt against their French slave-masters, and declared Haiti a free and independent island.

François Dominique Toussaint was born in about 1743 on the Caribbean island and French **colony** of St Domingue (now called Haiti). His father was the son of an African chief who had been captured and taken to St Domingue to work on a sugar plantation.

Plantation life

Toussaint was the oldest of eight brothers and sisters, all born into slavery on the plantation. Every day, Toussaint spent long hours cutting sugar cane, but he spent any free time trying to learn French, Latin and mathematics. His owner was a fair and honest man who could see that Toussaint was very bright. He tried to encourage Toussaint and gave him a responsible job looking after the animals on the estate.

A free man

In 1777, Toussaint was freed from slavery, but he knew how lucky he was. Many slaves were ill-treated by their owners. They were starved, and often beaten to try to force them to work harder. Some died as a result of this brutal treatment.

Slave leader Toussaint L'Ouverture in European military uniform. He **abolished** slavery on Haiti.

Slaves cutting down ripe sugar cane on a plantation. Many Europeans became very rich growing sugar in the Caribbean.

Slave revolt

In 1791, there was news of a rebellion on the island. The slaves had risen up in protest against their masters. The sugar cane fields were set on fire, and the plantation owners and their families murdered. Toussaint helped his master to escape, and then decided to join the rebels. He was immediately made leader of the rebel troops.

Rebel leader

Toussaint's education earned him the respect and admiration of the slaves. They gave him the name L'Ouverture, which means 'the opener of the way to freedom'.

The rebels were inspired by the success of the French Revolution, and the new society based on freedom and equality for all people. This helped to spur them on in their fight for freedom.

The Slave Trade

During the sixteenth and seventeenth centuries, millions of Africans were taken from their homes and transported to the Americas where they were forced to work as slaves. Many spent the rest of their lives working on cotton, tobacco and sugar plantations. Often slaves were chained together to make sure they could not escape. This slave is wearing a ring around his neck which made it impossible for him to lie down.

Governor general

Toussaint was a brilliant soldier, and under his leadership the rebels became a powerful fighting force. In 1793, Toussaint and his rebels joined forces with the French to fight off English and Spanish troops who were trying to invade St Domingue. Toussaint was rewarded for his bravery with the title of governor general of the island. He abolished slavery and, in 1801, declared St Domingue independent.

French invasion

But the French leader, Napoleon Bonaparte, wanted St Domingue back under French control. In 1802, he sent 20 000 troops to recapture the island. The French commander told Toussaint that no harm would come to him if he agreed to meet to discuss a peace settlement. But the commander broke his promise. Toussaint was arrested and taken back to France.

Toussaint's arrest by French army officers in 1802. Napoleon feared that Toussaint would organize an uprising against the French forces on St Domingue.

Napoleon Bonaparte

In 1804, Napoleon Bonaparte became Emperor of France. His ambition was to rule Europe, and he conquered Spain, Austria, Prussia and Italy before things started to go wrong. After a long war his army was defeated in Spain, and in 1812 he lost nearly half a million troops when he tried to attack Moscow. His men were unprepared for the bitterly cold Russian winter, and thousands froze to death. In 1815, Bonaparte was defeated at the battle of Waterloo, Belgium.

Imprisoned in France

Bonaparte did not want to start a rebellion on St Domingue by executing Toussaint. Instead he imprisoned the rebel leader in a prison called Fort-de-Joux, high in the French Alps. Toussaint became weaker and weaker as a result of lack of food and the freezing temperatures. On 7 April 1803, he was found dead in his cell.

Fight for freedom

Toussaint's followers were outraged when they heard about their leader's death. They rose up in revolt against the French troops on the island and, after a long and bloody battle, they finally defeated them. The rebels renamed their island Haiti. In 1804, Haiti was once again declared independent.

Independence again

Toussaint had foreseen this last, successful rebellion. When he was arrested and forced to board the boat to France he said, 'In overthrowing me, you have cut down in St Domingue only the trunk of the tree of liberty. It will spring up again by the roots for they are numerous and deep.'

Toussaint did not live to see his **prophecy** come true. But under his leadership, the slaves won their freedom, and Haiti became the first independent black country in the Caribbean.

Rebel slaves fighting French troops on Haiti. France could not believe that its army had been defeated by slaves.

GEORGES DANTON

1759–1794

One of the great leaders of the French Revolution was Georges Danton. He fought for reforms in French government and society, and sacrificed his life for his beliefs.

By the end of the eighteenth century, France was on the verge of revolution. The country was almost **bankrupt** as a result of three major wars. Food prices soared and wages dropped. French people struggled to pay their **taxes**, and buy enough bread to feed their families, while the King, Louis XVl, and his wife Marie Antoinette lived a life of luxury in their palace at **Versailles**. Louis refused to listen to his subjects' complaints. He held all political power and no one was allowed to criticize him.

A popular figure

Georges Danton was born in 1759. He studied law, and moved to Paris in 1785 to open a law practice. Like many other French people, Danton believed that the French government was **corrupt**. He criticized the king and called for reforms in the way France was governed. With his striking features and strong voice, Danton soon became a popular political figure.

Georges Danton was one of the first revolutionaries to call for an end to the French monarchy and the execution of Louis XVI in 1793.

French society

In spring 1789 rioting broke out. French men and women had risen up in rebellion against the king's demands for extra taxes. The French system of taxation was very unfair. The nobles and the clergy were the richest groups in French society, but they paid hardly any taxes. This meant that poor people paid the most tax.

Storming the Bastille

Events came to a head in Paris on 14 July 1789 when angry crowds marched to the Bastille in Paris. The Bastille was an ancient prison and a symbol of royal authority. The mob surged into the prison and killed the governor. They cut off his head, stuck it on a **pike** and carried it through the city.

The road to revolution

The revolutionaries adopted the slogan 'liberty, equality and fraternity'. They refused to recognize noble titles and called everyone citizen as a sign of equality. Danton emerged as one of the revolutionary leaders. He called for an end to the **privileges** of the French monarchy.

French citizens attacking the Bastille with guns and cannons.

The Estates-General

French society was divided into three groups called estates. The first was the clergy, the second was the nobility, and the Third Estate was everyone else from peasant farmers to businessmen. In May 1789, Louis XVI called the first meeting of the Estates-General since 1614. This meeting was a turning point. For the first time members of the Third Estate outnumbered the clergy and the nobility. This meant that the Third Estate had more power than ever before. The king tried to end the meeting, but the Third Estate refused to go home until France had a **constitution**.

The death of the king

In 1791, Louis tried to flee France to join his European **allies** who were fighting to crush the Revolution. But he was captured and taken back to face an angry mob in Paris. On 10 August 1792, Danton helped organize an uprising against the monarchy, and Louis and his family were imprisoned. France was declared a **republic**. In 1793, Louis XVI was beheaded by **guillotine**.

The revolutionary government

For three months, Danton was head of the new revolutionary government, which was called the Convention. But before long members of the Convention began to argue about how France should be run.

The execution of Louis XVI. The executioner holds the king's head up for the crowd to see.

Maximilien Robespierre

Maximilien Robespierre was one of the leaders of the French Revolution, but he is best remembered for his cruelty and ruthlessness. Robespierre ordered the execution of thousands of people he suspected of opposing the revolution. By the summer of 1794, many of Robespierre's colleagues were tired of his brutal **tyranny**. They rose against him, and he was executed by guillotine that same year.

Danton is led up the steps of the guillotine. He met his death bravely, making jokes and laughing with his supporters. Soldiers surrounded the guillotine to stop any attempts to rescue him.

The Reign of Terror

Danton's popularity and **moderate** views annoyed the **radical** revolutionaries, and by July 1793, Robespierre and his followers had taken control. The Reign of Terror followed. During this time, anyone who opposed the revolution was condemned to death. More than 300 000 people were arrested and 17 000 were executed.

Arrest and execution

Danton spoke out in public against the executions, and was promptly arrested. At his trial he was not allowed to defend himself or call any witnesses. On 4 April 1794, Danton was found guilty of plotting against the republic, and he was executed the following day. Danton's last words were to his executioner. He said, 'Be sure not to forget to show my head to the people! It is well worth seeing!'

Shock waves

Danton's death did not bring the French Revolution to an end. The conflict carried on for another five years until Napoleon Bonaparte seized power in 1799. But Danton did not die in vain.

News of the revolution sent shock waves throughout Europe and America. The old order of power, wealth and privilege had been destroyed forever, and replaced by a new society based on freedom and equality. All over the world, people living under **oppressive regimes** were encouraged to fight for changes in the way their countries were governed.

SIMÓN BOLÍVAR

1783-1830

During the nineteenth century, Simón Bolívar led the people of South America in their fight against Spanish rule. He became known as The Liberator, and Bolivia was named in his honour.

In the sixteenth century, Spain conquered large areas of South America. Spanish settlers bought farmland and communities grew up. By the end of the eighteenth century, much of South America was ruled by Spain. But most South Americans wanted independence; they hated working for the Spaniards, and being forced to pay high **taxes** to the Spanish government.

European influences

Simón Bolívar was born in 1783 in Caracas, the capital of Venezuela. His father was a wealthy cocoa planter, and Bolívar grew up in comfort on the family plantation.

In 1804, Bolívar travelled to Europe. The French Revolution of 1789 had made a great impact on European people, and Bolívar was excited by the new society based on freedom and equality. The idea of independence for Venezuela captured his imagination, and he vowed to return home and free his country from Spanish rule.

South American revolutionary hero Simón Bolívar. Under his leadership, Colombia, Peru, Venezuela and Ecuador gained independence.

The victorious soldier. Bolivar's dream was to unite all the countries of South America into one nation.

Bitter warfare

Bolívar crossed the border into Colombia, where he recruited more men. He led his new army back to Venezuela, where after six bloody and violent battles, the rebels recaptured Caracas. In August 1813, Bolívar rode triumphantly into the city, and declared Venezuela independent. He was named The Liberator, and became political leader of the country. But this was just the beginning of the war for independence.

Defeat in Caracas

By the time Bolívar returned to Venezuela the fight for freedom had already begun. The protesters formed a rebel army, and in 1810 they captured Caracas. But their success was shortlived. The rebels were not strong enough to fight off the Spanish army and they were soon defeated.

Military leader

In 1811, Bolívar became the military leader of the rebel army. Over the next two years, he plotted against the Spanish and fought many battles, but Spain was not going to give up its empire without a struggle.

Spanish rule

When the Spaniards settled in South America, they forced the local people to work for them. Many South Americans died because they were treated so badly and made to work long hours. Others died from diseases, such as smallpox, that the Spaniards brought with them from Europe.

Life in exile

Just one year later, Bolívar was once again defeated by the Spanish. He fled to Jamaica where he spent the next three years living in **exile**. He knew that his forces would never be able to defeat the Spanish army in open battle. So, instead he decided to use unusual tactics to trick them.

Joyful crowds line the streets of Caracas to welcome Simón Bolívar and his rebel army. The city was finally freed from Spanish rule in 1821, after the rebels won the Battle of Carabobo.

Spectacular tactics

With an army of 2500 foreign soldiers, Bolívar led an attack on Colombia. The men marched through forests, flooded rivers and over the icy Andes mountains which separate Venezuela and Colombia. This skilful campaign was a success. The rebels found the Spanish soldiers unprepared, and defeated them at the Battle of Boyaca in 1819. Later that year, Bolívar became President of Colombia.

The new president

In 1821, Bolívar freed his home of Venezuela. In 1822, he carried on the revolution in other parts of South America, and freed Ecuador and Panama from Spanish rule. A new state was created called the republic of Gran Colombia. It was a **federation** of present-day Venezuela, Colombia, Panama and Ecuador, and Bolívar was its president. Peru was the last country to be liberated, but by 1825 Spanish power was brought to an end. Upper Peru was called Bolivia, in honour of Simón Bolívar.

Rousseau

Jean-Jacques Rousseau was a Swiss **philosopher** who wrote many books criticizing the society of eighteenth-century France. His works, which said that all men and women were born free and equal, inspired Simón Bolívar to free South America from Spanish rule. Rousseau's work was not popular with the French authorities, and he was forced to live in exile for many years.

A Republican Confederation

Bolívar hoped to make all the countries he had liberated into one rich and powerful state. But, gradually, people began to distrust him, believing that he wanted too much power. One by one the new independent states broke away from Gran Colombia, until only Colombia remained in the federation. Even the people of his homeland, Venezuela, rebelled against him.

The *Independence* **Mural** (1960) by Juan O'Gorman. The mural celebrates the achievements of Simón Bolívar who is shown in uniform on the far left.

Resignation from office

Bolívar was deeply hurt when he saw the countries he had liberated turn against him. He resigned as President of Colombia in 1830, and made plans to live the rest of his life in Europe. But this was not to be. Simón Bolívar died near Santa Marta on the coast of Colombia in December 1830.

A great legacy

Simón Bolívar is remembered as South America's greatest liberator. Despite the fact that he was unable to hold his **republic** together, he helped to unite the people of South America in their struggle against their common enemy, Spain.

GERONIMO

1829–1909

Unlike most revolutionaries who fight to bring about change, Geronimo fought to protect the Native American way of life from the might of the United States army.

North America was once populated by Native American peoples. Each Native American nation had its own customs and laws, and the people shared the land and lived in harmony with their environment. Wild animals, such as deer and buffalo, were plentiful and provided meat, clothing and tools, which were made from the animals' bones. The Native Americans also ate fish, and crops grown on their small plots of land.

European settlers

Throughout the nineteenth century, thousands and eventually millions of people **emigrated** to America from Europe. They all took land from the Native Americans, often claiming to have bought it in exchange for a few trinkets. The European settlers killed the buffalo, and tried to convert the Native Americans to Christianity. The Native Americans' traditional way of life was changed forever.

Geronimo, one of the most famous Apache warriors. His raids on the American army were so successful that people thought he had supernatural powers.

Reservation lands

In 1830, the Indian Removal Act forced all Native Americans to move to reservations. These were small areas of land which were set aside by the American government for the Native Americans. Often the reservations were on poor, barren land. Those Native Americans who refused to move were rounded up and escorted by the American army. Many Native Americans died before they reached the reservations.

The Apaches

Geronimo was a member of the Chiricahua Apaches. He was born in 1829 in No-Doyohn Canyon. Today, this site is in Arizona, USA, but when Geronimo was born it was owned by Mexico. Geronimo was his Mexican nickname. His Apache name was Goyathlay, or 'he who yawns'.

Guerrilla warfare

Geronimo fought against the **colonization** of his lands by the European settlers, but it was not until 1861 that the troubles really began. In that year, the American army hanged three Apaches. For the next 25 years, the Apaches fought a **guerrilla** campaign against the army in which more people were killed than in any other Native American war.

An Apache ambush.

On the move

In 1876, the American government forced the Chiricahuas to move from Mexico to a dry, dusty reservation at San Carlos in eastern Arizona. Geronimo refused to go, and led a breakaway group of Apaches into Mexico. They were free for over a year, before they were tracked down by the army and taken back to the reservation.

Rumours of arrest

For the next four years, the Chiricahuas lived peacefully on the reservation. But then they heard rumours that the American government was planning to arrest and kill all the Apache leaders who had opposed the army.

Peace talks

On hearing the news, Geronimo and a band of warriors fled back to a secret hiding place in the Sierra Madre Mountains in Mexico. The American government knew that it would be hard to win a guerrilla war in the mountains. So, in 1882 General Crook was sent to **negotiate** with the Apaches. Crook had fought the Apaches many times and had a great respect for them. Crook told Geronimo that if the Apaches returned to Arizona the government would treat them fairly.

A photograph taken in 1886 showing Geronimo and General Crook negotiating peace terms.

Native Americans today

In 1952, the reservations were **abolished**, and Native Americans were free to live where they pleased. Today, many Native Americans are negotiating with the government for the return of their lands, or for **financial compensation**. Others have set up **roadblocks** to try to reclaim land that they believe the government stole. At the same time Native Americans all over the USA are learning the native languages, dances and other traditional skills of their ancestors. They are making sure that their ancient customs are not forgotten.

The Apaches are out!

Geronimo wanted to believe Crook, and the Apaches returned to the reservation. But the government leaders broke their promise, and demanded that Geronimo be hanged. The Chiricahuas were outraged at this betrayal, and Geronimo took flight along with 35 men, 8 boys and 101 women. American newspapers reported the event under the headline 'The Apaches Are Out!'

Geronimo surrenders

This time the government was no longer prepared to negotiate. In 1886, General Crook was replaced by a brutal and unsympathetic soldier whose mission was to capture or kill Geronimo. Throughout the summer of that year, Geronimo and his warriors were chased by 5000 American soldiers and thousands of volunteers. The Apaches were eventually trapped in the Mexican mountains where they surrendered.

Prisoner of war

Geronimo and his warriors were taken to Florida where they were forced to work as labourers. The American goverment treated the Apaches harshly. Geronimo was not allowed to see his family for more than a year. He remained a **prisoner of war** for the rest of his life, and never saw his homeland again. Geronimo died in 1909.

Today, Geronimo is seen as a hero – a brave warrior who fought the American government for the freedom of the Native American peoples.

EMMA GOLDMAN

1869–1940

International **anarchist** Emma Goldman devoted her life to a passionate belief in the freedom of the individual, and a struggle against all forms of injustice.

Emma Goldman was born in 1869 to Jewish parents living in Lithuania, which was part of the Russian empire. Her childhood was very unhappy. Her family was poor, and Emma's father often beat her. As Emma grew up she became aware of the **persecution** of Jews in Russia. Young boys aged 12 were forced into the army and made to serve for 30 years. Other Jews were beaten until they gave up their faith and converted to Christianity. It was this background that formed Emma Goldman's determination to fight injustice.

Running away to America

When she was 16, Goldman's father tried to force her into an **arranged marriage**. But she ran away and **emigrated** to the United States of America with her half-sister, Helena. The sisters lived in New York State, and Goldman found work in a clothing factory. In 1887, she married a fellow Russian immigrant, Jacob Kershner, but the marriage ended in divorce.

American anarchist Emma Goldman. In 1903, the American government passed a law to **deport** all anarchists living in the USA.

The Haymarket Anarchists

In 1886, Goldman read about the trial of the Haymarket Anarchists in Chicago. These eight men, who believed in greater rights for working people, were accused of throwing a bomb at police in Haymarket Square. Only two of the men had been present when the bomb exploded, but they were all found guilty. Four of the anarchists were hanged on 11 November 1887.

Moving to New York City

Goldman sympathized with the anarchists. She, too, believed in better conditions and higher wages for workers. She decided to move to New York City so that she could meet other people who shared her beliefs. In New York Goldman met Alexander Berkman, a Russian anarchist, who became her life-long friend.

The Haymarket bomb explosion. The bomb was thrown after police broke up an anarchist meeting.

Assassination attempt

In 1892, Goldman and Berkman plotted to **assassinate** Henry Frick, a wealthy steel tycoon. Frick had tried to cut wages at one of his steel plants, and the workers had gone on strike. Fighting broke out and several workers were killed. But Berkman's attack failed and he was sentenced to 22 years imprisonment.

Emigration to America

People emigrate when they move from one country to another with the intention of settling there. Between 1815 and 1860, about five million immigrants entered the USA. This rose to over eight million in the first ten years of the twentieth century. Many immigrants, or their **descendants**, living in the USA today are from Britain, Germany, Scandinavia, the Mediterranean and eastern Europe.

Red Emma

Goldman became known as Red Emma because of her **radical** views. In 1893, she was jailed for two years for starting a riot in New York. After her release from prison, Goldman lectured throughout America and Europe. She spoke out against the American government, and the poor working conditions and low wages that many workers had to suffer.

But this life soon came to a halt. In 1901, William McKinley, the President of the USA, was assassinated by an anarchist. Goldman was questioned by police, not because there was any evidence against her, but because she was an anarchist.

Anarchism

Anarchism is a political theory based on the idea that people do not need a government to rule them. Instead, communities and individuals work together to provide goods and services. One of the most famous anarchists is Pierre-Joseph Proudhon (1809-65) who wanted a society without government.

Mother Earth

There was such an angry public reaction against anarchism that Goldman went into hiding. She had to keep her activities secret, but in 1906 she published a journal called *Mother Earth*. In it, she wrote about **feminism**, women's rights and birth control. People were so horrified by the journal that Goldman was imprisoned for outraging public opinion.

Russian exile

Goldman was against America's involvement in the **First World War** (1914-18), and in 1917 she was sentenced to five years' imprisonment for encouraging people to resist **conscription**. After two years in prison, she was deported to Russia where she served the rest of her sentence.

Goldman was never allowed to return to live in the USA. Instead, she spent the rest of her life travelling and lecturing all over Europe and Canada.

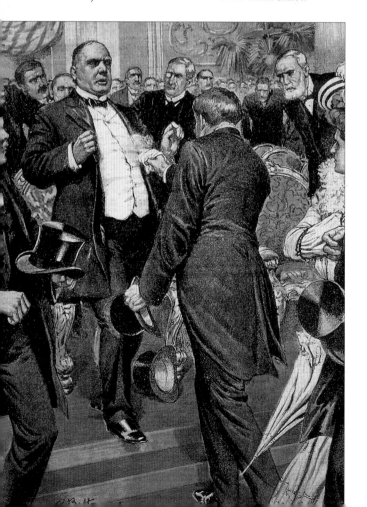

On 6 September 1901, President McKinley was assassinated by a Polish anarchist, Leon Czolgosz. After the shooting, anarchists all over the USA were arrested.

A New York City tenement building around 1900. Immigrant families often lived together in one building, which was divided into apartments.

A better society

In 1931, Goldman published her autobiography, *Living My Life*, in which she tried to show how society could change for the better. Five years after, Alexander Berkman committed suicide, but Goldman carried on with her work. She continued to write, and published works on anarchism, feminism and birth control. Emma Goldman died in 1940 of a heart attack. She was buried beside the Haymarket Martyrs in Chicago.

A passionate struggle

For most of her life, Emma Goldman chose to go her own way without thinking of her own safety and comfort. She believed in freedom, equality and justice for everyone. She once said, 'I will bow to nothing except my idea of right'.

Alexander Berkman, life-long friend of Emma Goldman and American anarchist.

VLADIMIR LENIN

1870-1924

In 1922, Vladimir Lenin, Russian revolutionary and founder of Russian **Communism**, became the leader of the largest country in the world, the Union of Soviet Socialist Republics (USSR).

Lenin, whose original name was Vladimir Ilyich Ulyanov, was born in 1870 in the city of Simbirsk on the River Volga, Russia. He was the son of a school inspector and had five brothers and sisters. Lenin's family lived in comfort, but there were many poor people in Russia. The poorest were the **serfs** who were almost like slaves. The serfs and the peasants were always in debt because **taxes** were so high and the farmland they rented was so expensive.

Blaming the tsar

Many people blamed the tsar, or Russian emperor, for their poverty. While millions of Russians worked long hours in factories for very low wages, the tsar and the wealthy ruling classes lived in luxury.

Opposition against the tsar grew. Many ordinary people wanted to fight for better conditions. In 1887, Lenin's older brother was executed for trying to kill Tsar Alexander III. This incident made Lenin more aware of the problems in his country.

Vladimir Lenin, leader of the Russian Revolution and first head of state of the USSR.

An interest in politics

In 1887, Lenin went to the University of Kazan to study law, but he was expelled for taking part in a student protest meeting. He was not allowed to return to the university to finish his studies, so instead Lenin spent his time reading the works of political thinkers, such as Karl Marx. In 1889, Lenin and his family moved to Samara, where he was allowed to take his law exams.

Exile to Siberia

Lenin practised law until 1893, but he continued his political activities, and was soon in trouble with the authorities. In 1897, he was imprisoned for **subversive** behaviour and **exiled** to Siberia, where he took the name Lenin from the River Lena.

Karl Marx

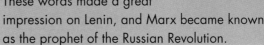

Karl Marx was a German **philosopher** who wrote *The Communist Manifesto*. This work ended with the words 'the workers have nothing to lose but their chains. They have a world to win. Workers of all countries, unite!' These words made a great impression on Lenin, and Marx became known as the prophet of the Russian Revolution.

The Bolsheviks

In 1898, the Russian Social Democratic Workers' Party was formed. Lenin became the leader of the **militant** wing of the party, the Bolsheviks, which means 'members of the majority'. Lenin wanted major reforms in the way Russia was governed. He said that land should be the property of the people and the factories and banks should be owned by the Russian state.

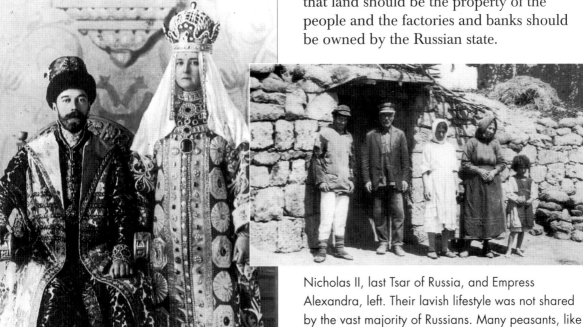

Nicholas II, last Tsar of Russia, and Empress Alexandra, left. Their lavish lifestyle was not shared by the vast majority of Russians. Many peasants, like those above, lived in very primitive conditions.

In 1917, the Bolsheviks stormed the Winter Palace. The capture of the tsar's royal palace was proof that the workers' revolution had finally succeeded.

Massacre at the Winter Palace

Lenin began to organize action against the government. On 22 January 1905, 200 000 people marched towards the Winter Palace, the home of Tsar Nicholas II and symbol of royal authority. They wanted the tsar to listen to their complaints about high taxes and long hours spent working in factories.

But the demonstrators were attacked by the tsar's army. The soldiers rode straight into the crowd, striking out with their swords at men, women and children. Other troops fired on the demonstrators as they tried to escape. The bodies of the dead and wounded lay all around the Winter Palace, and the snow was stained red with their blood. Lenin fled Russia and spent the next 12 years living in exile in Switzerland.

The returning hero

Lenin returned to Russia in March 1917. He arrived in St Petersburg, (renamed Petrograd) to a hero's welcome. Lenin called for a revolution to put a Bolshevik government into power. His forceful personality and stirring speeches persuaded thousands of factory workers, soldiers and sailors to follow his call. The Bolsheviks organized huge demonstrations against the government and the tsar was forced to give up his throne. In 1918, the tsar and his family were killed by revolutionaries.

The October Revolution

During 1917, the Bolsheviks set up their headquarters in Petrograd. Soon they had taken control of key points in the city, such as the railway stations. On 23 October 1917, Lenin and his followers attacked and captured the Winter Palace. The Bolsheviks seized power and, with Lenin as the head of government, they took control of Russia. The Bolshevik Party was renamed the Russian Communist Party.

The first Communist revolution

In 1922, the old Russian empire became the Union of Soviet Socialist Republics (USSR), or the Soviet Union, and Lenin became the ruler of the largest country in the world. But in 1924, just two years after he came to power, Lenin died. Five days after his death, Petrograd was renamed Leningrad in his honour.

The Russian Revolution ended 400 years of rule by the Russian tsars. Lenin led the revolt and masterminded the first successful Communist revolution. The Communist Party stayed in power until the 1990s.

Russia suffered enormous losses during the First World War (1914-18). By 1917, many soldiers were tired of the conflict. They joined the Bolsheviks, and demonstrated against the tsar and his government.

Rasputin

Rasputin, seated far left, was a Siberian peasant who became a priest. In 1905, he met the Russian royal family and persuaded the Empress Alexandra that he was able to cure her son, Alexei, of a rare disease called **haemophilia**.

Rasputin became very powerful and Empress Alexandra quickly fell under his evil influence. He is partly blamed for the tsar's failure to listen to his people's complaints, which led to the Russian Revolution. Rasputin was murdered in 1916 by a group of Russian nobles.

EMILIANO ZAPATA

1879-1919

Mexican revolutionary
Emiliano Zapata
was the leader of
a peasant uprising that forced
wealthy Mexican landowners
to return stolen land to the people.

Between 1876 and 1910, a ruthless **dictator** called Porfirio Díaz ruled Mexico. Díaz was supported by the owners of the haciendas. These were the big estates where the wealthy landowners lived. Díaz gave the owners land in return for their continued support.

Life on the land

The landowners employed local peasants to work on the estates. But the peasants, who were mostly Native Americans, were treated badly and forced to work like slaves. Some died of starvation. Many peasants had once owned small farms, but their land had been taken by the government and given to the haciendas.

Horse trader

Emiliano Zapata was born in 1879 in a peasant village in the state of Morelos, southern Mexico. When he was just 17, Zapata's parents died leaving him to look after his brothers and sisters. He supported his family by training and selling horses.

Emiliano Zapata, Mexican **guerrilla** fighter and revolutionary leader in 1913.

Pancho Villa

Pancho Villa was a Mexican bandit and freedom fighter who controlled his own guerrilla army. During the Mexican Revolution, Villa sometimes went to the aid of Zapata and his rebel army.

Villa's exploits made him a folk hero throughout Mexico. When he was a young man, Villa is said to have killed his boss' son. Pancho Villa eventually made his peace with the Mexican government, only to be **assassinated** in 1923 by one of his old enemies.

Village protest

In 1897, the peasants in Zapata's village organized a protest against the local landowner who had taken their land. Zapata joined in, and was arrested by the local authorities. Before long he had a reputation as a troublemaker.

Growing discontent

Zapata was drafted into the army for six months. When he returned to Morelos, his neighbours elected him president of the board of defence for their village. They wanted him to help them fight the landowners.

Peasant movement

In 1909, Zapata and his neighbours chased the local landowner off his estate. The peasants took over the hacienda and shared out the land among themselves. News of the protest spread. Other villages joined the rebels, and they formed a rebel army.

A Mexican wood carving showing peasants being driven from their farms by the landowners.

Francisco Madero

In 1910, Díaz was overthrown, and Francisco Madero, another wealthy landowner, was elected president of Mexico. Madero promised Zapata that he would return land to the peasants, but once he was in power he went back on his promise. Zapata was very angry and accused Madero of betrayal.

Zapata adopted the slogan 'Land and Liberty'. Under his leadership, the peasants waged a bloody and often violent campaign against the landowners.

Rebel army

Support for the rebels continued to grow, and Zapata found himself the leader of 70 000 landless men and women. The rebels were organized in small guerrilla bands. They ambushed the government troops sent to stop the revolt, and then went back to their villages where they buried their rifles under the mud floor of their huts. When the soldiers entered the villages, all they saw were peasants ploughing their tiny parcels of land. By 1911, Zapata's forces controlled the state of Morelos. During the fight, the Mexican bandit Pancho Villa often went to help Zapata and his rebel army.

Members of Zapata's ragged rebel army capture a train at Morelos, southern Mexico.

Diego Rivera's mosaic **mural** (1953) was commissioned to celebrate Zapata and the Mexican Revolution of 1910.

Political rivals

Zapata lived with a price on his head throughout these difficult and dangerous years, but the peasants were passionately loyal, and nobody within his movement was tempted to betray him. Zapata was eventually betrayed by his political rivals. He was tricked into going to a secret meeting with a government official who said he wanted to join the peasant movement. Zapata rode to the meeting place, and was immediately shot dead by soldiers who were waiting to ambush him.

The revolution continues

The Mexican Revolution continued after Emiliano Zapata's death, and it was not until the 1930s that the peasants were able to enjoy the benefits of the land reforms that he had fought for.

A national hero

Since his death, Emiliano Zapata has become one of Mexico's national heroes. His famous words 'It is better to die on your feet than live on your knees!' inspired the men and women of southern Mexico to rise up and join him in his fight to give land back to the people.

Zapata's white horse

Zapata's white horse was famous all over southern Mexico because of its pure white colour. Zapata was riding the horse on the day he was ambushed and shot. His killers wanted to capture the horse to stop the legend of its famous rider from growing. But the horse got away. Thousands of Mexicans believed that Zapata's spirit escaped with his horse.

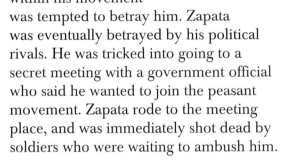

MICHAEL COLLINS

1890–1922

In the early years of the twentieth century, Michael Collins led the Irish struggle for independence from British control. He is considered to be one of the greatest revolutionaries in Irish history.

Michael Collins was born in West Cork, Ireland in 1890. When he was 16 years old, Collins, like many other young Irish men, **emigrated** to England in search of work. He eventually found a job as a clerk in the London branch of an American bank.

Independent rule

At this time, Ireland was part of Great Britain, but a growing number of Irish people wanted to break away. They felt they were treated unfairly by the British government. England was becoming wealthy and industrialized, while Ireland was still a **rural society** with little industry. Collins was a strong supporter of home rule for Ireland. During his time in London he joined a secret society called the Irish Republican Brotherhood. The members of the society were ready to fight to make Ireland a **republic**.

Irish Republican leader Michael Collins in military uniform. Collins became famous as chief planner of the revolutionary movement. He was one of the most wanted men in Britain.

Rebellion and imprisonment

Collins returned to Ireland in 1916, in time to take part in the Easter Rising. This rebellion was organized by republicans in Dublin who wanted immediate Irish independence from Britain. The rebellion failed, but the cruel treatment of the rebel leaders brought the republican struggle to the attention of the Irish people.

Collins was arrested and imprisoned along with other republicans, including Eamon de Valera. The rebels were released in December 1916, and de Valera became the leader of the Irish Republican Party, Sinn Fein, which means 'ourselves alone'.

An Irish parliament

In 1918, Sinn Fein won 27 seats in the British general election. Michael Collins was one of the newly elected members of parliament (MP). But the Sinn Fein MPs refused to go to **parliament** in London. They set up their own parliament in Dublin, and declared Ireland independent.

Between 1919 and 1921, members of Sinn Fein were held in prison in Ireland.

The Irish Republican Army

From 1919 to 1921, there was bitter fighting between the British government and the Irish republicans, and many people were killed or injured. Collins became director of Sinn Fein's military wing, later to be called the Irish Republican Army (IRA). He led this organization so successfully that the British government offered a £10,000 reward for his capture.

The Easter Rising

On Easter Monday, 1916, Irish republicans in Dublin rose in armed revolt against British rule. Many buildings were destroyed, including the General Post Office in Dublin, shown here. The rebellion was crushed within a week, leaving 100 British soldiers and 450 Irish rebels dead. Fourteen rebel leaders were executed, which gained public sympathy, and many Irish people declared their support for the republicans.

Thousands of people gathered to hear Michael Collins launch the Irish Free State in Dublin in 1922. Collins tried to win support for the new state, but many republicans refused to accept it.

The Anglo-Irish Treaty

In July 1921, Collins decided to **negotiate** with the British government rather than carry on fighting. On 6 December 1921, after months of difficult and sometimes **deadlocked** negotiations, an agreement known as the Anglo-Irish Treaty was signed between the British government and the Irish Republican Party. The treaty made most of Ireland independent, but left Northern Ireland under British rule. The newly independent provinces were called the Irish Free State. In 1949, the Irish Free State became the Republic of Ireland.

A divided party

Collins knew that the treaty would not be acceptable to many republicans because part of Ireland remained under British control. Some republicans felt he had betrayed the cause. After signing the treaty, Collins is reported to have said 'I have signed my death warrant'.

Eamon de Valera

Eamon de Valera, (far right) inspecting IRA troops. De Valera was one of the leaders of the Irish struggle for home rule. He supported the anti-treaty republicans who felt that Ireland should not be **partitioned**. De Valera started a party called Fianna Fail (Warriors of Ireland). The party won the 1932 general election, and De Valera was elected Prime Minister.

Men of the South (1921) by Sean Keating.
The painting shows a band of IRA volunteers
preparing for battle.

The Irish civil war

Michael Collins became chairman of the
new **provisional government**. But many
republicans, including De Valera, were so
strongly opposed to the treaty that **civil
war** broke out between the anti-treaty
republicans and the new government.

Military inspection

On 22 August 1922, Michael Collins
was in Cork inspecting military operations.
The car he was driving was forced to
stop because there were obstacles in the
road. When the car stopped, Collins
was ambushed and shot dead by
anti-treaty republicans.

Natural leader

Michael Collins was a natural leader with
a forceful personality and great energy.
He did not live to see an independent
Ireland, but he made a great contribution
to the Irish struggle for self-government.

MAO ZEDONG

1893–1976

Mao Zedong, Chairman of the People's Republic of China, united China under the rule of the **Communist Party**. At the height of his power, Mao was the leader of more than a quarter of the world's population.

For over 3000 years until the beginning of the twentieth century, China was an **empire**. In 1912, the emperor was forced to **abdicate**, and China became a **republic** ruled over by a president. But soon rival **warlords** and their private armies split the country between them and fought for power. The Nationalist Party under the leadership of Chiang Kai-shek defeated the warlords, and Chiang became ruler of China in 1928.

The young rebel

Mao was born in 1893. According to Chinese astrology, this was the year of the Black Snake, and Mao was born in the hour of the Green Dragon. These were signs that his life would be full of blood and violence. Even as a child Mao was a rebel. When he should have been working in the fields, he spent his time talking to the local villagers, and reading romantic stories about life in old China.

A photograph of Mao Zedong taken during the Long March in 1935. Mao helped found the Communist Party in China.

A Chinese boatwoman and her child in 1900.

Communist massacre

At first, the Communist Party worked with the Nationalist government. But as more and more Chinese joined the Communist Party, Chiang Kai-shek started to fear that the Communists would turn against him. In 1927, he ordered the massacre of thousands of Communists.

Mao escaped the massacre, and he fled along with other survivors to a base in the middle of China. But the Nationalist troops followed them and continued their attacks. Mao knew that the Communists had no choice but to move again. He took them on a journey of about 9700 km to a new base in northern China. This epic journey is known as the Long March.

Joining the Communist Party

Mao went to teacher training college, where he became interested in politics. In 1921, he was one of the first members of the new Chinese Communist Party, and in 1923 he became a full-time party worker. The Communists wanted reforms in government so that all land and property was owned by the state for the people.

Japanese invasion

In 1937, China was invaded by Japan. The Nationalist government found it impossible to resist the Japanese forces, and Chiang Kai-shek and his army retreated to the mountains, leaving the people to fend for themselves.

The Long March

In 1934, Mao led 100 000 Communists, including 35 women and a few children, on the Long March to Shaanxi Province to escape the Nationalist forces. The journey was very dangerous. The marchers climbed 18 mountain ranges, crossed 24 rivers, and trudged through deserts and swamps. After 568 days they arrived at their destination, but at a great cost. About 80 000 men and nearly all the women and children died on the way.

Japanese troops coming under attack in Shanghai during the Japanese-Chinese war.

People's liberation army

Mao sent his 'people's liberation army' into the villages that were occupied by the Japanese. The peasants could see that the Communists were prepared to help them, while the Nationalists had deserted them.

The growth of the party

When the Japanese left China in 1945, the Chinese people were very grateful to Mao. Membership of the Communist Party grew quickly, and Mao became a popular leader. His next plan was to overthrow the Nationalist government. There was civil war between the Communists and the Nationalists for three years until the Nationalists were defeated.

China's leader

In 1949, Mao's army captured Beijing, China's capital, and set up the Communist People's Republic of China. Mao became chairman of the party and leader of a quarter of the world's population.

Mao's government made important changes in China. Health care improved, as did standards of education. Many Chinese people could not read or write, and schools were set up so that children and adults could learn. Mao also improved conditions for women, so that for the first time they had equal rights with men.

The Cultural Revolution

The Cultural Revolution taught millions of young Chinese to destroy the 'Four Olds': old thinking, old culture, old customs and old habits. Many older people were abused and criticized. Universities, factories and even hospitals were closed while young and inexperienced students attacked older staff. University teachers were forced to leave their homes and work on the land. Everyone was given a copy of the *Little Red Book*, which was a collection of Mao's thoughts and sayings.

China's leap forward

Gradually China's economy improved, but Mao was not satisfied. He wanted a rapid increase in agricultural and industrial production. He planned a great economic revolution, which became known the Great Leap Forward. But the government did not invest enough money in new technology, and bad weather ruined many crops resulting in severe food shortages. Mao's influence weakened, and in 1959 he retired as chairman.

Return to power

In 1966, seven years after his retirement, Mao made a dramatic return to power to start the Cultural Revolution. This movement aimed to keep China free from the influences of the outside world. But it was also Mao's chance to take charge again and rid the Communist Party of members who had dared to disobey him. The Cultural Revolution lasted for ten years until Chairman Mao's death in 1976.

Economic growth

Under Mao's leadership, China became one of the most powerful countries in the world. But the price was high. The Cultural Revolution was a disaster. About one million people were killed, and many more were **exiled**, for simply disagreeing with the thoughts and actions of Chairman Mao.

A Chinese poster showing the Russian people's admiration for Chairman Mao.

GLOSSARY

Abdicate To give up the throne of a country.

Abolish To put an end to something, for example slavery.

Allies Countries that have agreed to support each other.

Anarchism A belief that people do not need a government or laws to live by.

Arranged marriage A marriage arranged for a boy and girl by their families.

Assassinate To murder a person by a surprise attack.

Bankrupt To have lost all money.

Civil war A war fought between people within the same country.

Colonies Land that is settled by people from another part of the world.

Colonization The act of setting up a colony, or community.

Communist Someone who believes that all people should be equal and that there should be no private ownership of land or industry.

Constitution A system of laws and customs to help govern the country.

Corrupt Dishonest and open to bribes.

Creditor Someone to whom money is owed.

Deadlocked A disagreement or problem that has become so complicated that it cannot be solved.

Deport To send away from a country.

Descendants The offspring or heirs to a family.

Economy The wealth of a country.

Emigrate To leave one country for another.

Empire A group of different countries ruled by the same state.

Exile To force a person to leave his or her home or country.

Federation A group of countries or states.

Feminism The belief that women should have the same rights as men.

Financial compensation To make amends for loss by paying money.

First World War The war between 1914-18 in which Britain, France, Russia and their allies defeated Germany, Austria-Hungary, and Turkey.

Guerrilla A fighter who wages war by ambush and surprise attack.

Guillotine An instrument with a single heavy blade for beheading people.

Haemophilia A disease in which blood loses its ability to clot, so that even a small wound can lead to fatal bleeding.

Militant The use of violence to further a cause.

Moderate A reasonable and usual view.

Mural A large picture on a wall.

Negotiate To talk with others in order to reach an agreement.

Oppressive regime A brutal and unjust system of government.

Parliament An assembly of people who pass the laws of a country.

Partition To divide a state into separate parts.

Persecution To harass, imprison or execute people for their political or religious opinions.

Pike A weapon like a spear.

Pioneer A person who is one of the first to settle in a new country.

Prisoner of war A member of an armed force captured during a war.

Privilege A benefit or advantage granted to a small group of people.

Prophecy To predict that something might happen in the future.

Provisional government A temporary administration of a country.

Radical An extreme political view.

Republic A state governed by the people or their elected representatives, not by a king or queen.

Roadblock An obstruction put across a road to stop traffic.

Rural society A community of people in the countryside.

Subversive Attempting to overthrow a government.

Tarred and feathered To smear someone with tar and cover them with feathers.

Taxes Money which people have to pay to the government.

Tyranny A cruel and illegal government or power.

Versailles The palace where the French royal family lived.

Warlords The military commanders of an independent army inside a country.

INDEX